disc

This book should be returned on or before the due date.

COUNTRYSIDE BOOKS
3 Catherine Road
Newbury, Berkshire

To view our complete range of books,
please visit us at
www.countrysidebooks.co.uk

ISBN 978 1 84674 350 4

Photographs by Catherine Smith
Cover design by Barrie Appleby

Designed by KT Designs, St Helens
Produced through The Letterworks Ltd., Reading
Typeset by KT Designs, St Helens
Printed in Poland

Introduction

Walking for pleasure is more than just a hobby, and so much more than mere exercise. It creates a peaceful state of mind, whilst exposing you to nature's calming elements. Whether it be in rain, wind or sunshine, there's always something worthwhile about being outside and escaping from life's daily grind.

And although a long, demanding walk can, at the time, feel challenging and tiring, there's a great sense of achievement at the end of it – particularly when you sit down in that cosy pub for a well-earned home-cooked meal. Many of the pubs chosen for this book have won awards for their good food, and they have open fires and lovely gardens so they can be enjoyed all year round.

Lincolnshire is a county that offers many diverse walks. There is the 80-mile coastline, the woods in the Wolds, the hills in the vales, the marshes of the fens, the dozens of canals and rivers to amble alongside, and the great Humber estuary to explore. Not all counties offer the variety that Lincolnshire can. To drive out to many of these walks does not require vast, busy motorways, but simple roads that run through the Lincolnshire countryside.

The maps in this book are very basic and I would always suggest you take the relevant OS map with you. Rights of way and public footpaths can change and may require you to take a detour. The use of fields can also change.

It's also a fact that many country pubs have irregular opening times. Some will open all day, whilst others may not open at lunchtimes. Always check in advance if you intend to dine there, and remember that Sunday lunchtime is very popular, so book ahead.

A final word from me. Walking makes you happy, a fact that has been medically proven. It's an activity that can be easily enjoyed and costs very little, yet benefits you greatly. I would like to thank my various companions who joined me, Hannah and her dog, Petal, Judith and her dog, Jazz, Ian and his old soldier, Hamlet. And, of course, my devoted cocker, Gracie, who happily posed for the photographs, even when I didn't want her to.

But most of all, my heart goes out to the 'old soldier', who sadly at aged 15 made this his last book, but found so much joy and happiness in our long adventures together. Hamlet, you were the perfect walking companion.

Catherine Smith

Publisher's Note

We hope that you obtain considerable enjoyment from this book: great care has been taken in its preparation. However, changes of landlord and actual pub closures are sadly not uncommon. Likewise, although at the time of publication all routes followed public rights of way or permitted paths, diversion orders can be made and permissions withdrawn.

We cannot, of course, be responsible for such diversion orders and any inaccuracies in the text which result from these or any other changes to the routes, nor any damage which might result from walkers trespassing on private property. We are anxious though that all details covering the walks and the pubs are kept up to date and would therefore welcome information from readers which would be relevant to future editions.

The simple sketch maps that accompany the walks in this book are based on notes made by the author whilst surveying the routes on the ground. They are designed to show you how to reach the start and to point out the main features of the overall circuit, and they contain a progression of numbers that relate to the paragraphs of the text.

However, for the benefit of a proper map, we do recommend that you purchase the relevant Ordnance Survey sheet covering your walk. Ordnance Survey maps are widely available, especially through booksellers and local newsagents.

To get in touch visit our website: www.countrysidebooks.co.uk

The Olive Branch, Clipsham.

The Humber Bridge.

1 South Ferriby and the Humber

4.9 miles (7.9 km)

WALK HIGHLIGHTS
Start with a gentle stroll along the embankment of the River Humber, taking in views of the mighty Humber Bridge before climbing up the Viking Way to the hilly peaks of South Ferriby and Horkstow. The walk finishes along the New River Ancholme, popular with canal boat and barge owners.

THE PUB
The Hope & Anchor, South Ferriby, **DN18 6JQ**
This lovely pub sits on the banks of the River Humber and was Lincolnshire's winner of Best Pub of Year 2017. There are wood burners in winter and outside decking with estuary views for the summer.
☎ 01652 635334 www.thehopeandanchorpub.co.uk

Guide to Lincolnshire Pub Walks

HOW TO GET THERE AND PARKING: From junction 5 of the M180, follow the A15 towards Barton upon Humber. Take the A1077 towards South Ferriby which sits on Sluice Road. Opposite the marina is the Hope and Anchor car park. **Sat nav** DN18 6JQ. If you decide to make the pub the halfway point instead, start at point 3 on Cliff Road. Off-road parking is available further up. **Sat nav** DN18 6RA.

MAP: OS Explorer 281 Ancholme Valley (GR SE 976211).

THE WALK

1 From the pub car park, turn left onto the pavement and cross the metal bridge. Directly afterwards is a wooden signpost for Humber Bank. Follow this short trail, bearing right towards the River Humber.

2 Continue along this estuary walk, taking in views of the mighty Humber Bridge stretching from Lincolnshire to Yorkshire. Along this stretch, you pass the South Ferriby Bird Hide and Fulseas Pumping Station as you continue in the direction of the Humber Bridge. You also pass South Ferriby Hall, built in 1805 for Sir John Nelthorpe. At the end of this section, the path leads you to bear right and climb a few steps into a field.

3 Walk directly ahead, with the hedge line on your right, and climb steadily towards a blue bench at the top with lovely views across the vast river. Turn right onto the Viking Way passing South Ferriby Hall again. The road passes some houses on Cliff Road and also 'The Horse Pond' as you reach a road junction. Cross this busy road (A1077) heading directly opposite Ferriby Hill, where there is a signpost, 'Piggery Hill', and a Viking Way marker.

4 This section is a steady climb up a windy track. When you reach the first bench, St Nicholas church is opposite and can be accessed by the gap in the hedge. It sits on a very sloping site and is thought to be smaller than it was originally due to landslides in the 19th century. Further along this road you pass a chalk pit quarry on your left. This is connected to the cement factory beside the Ferriby Sluice Marina on your right down the hill. Continue ahead, following the Viking Way and head towards the double pylons.

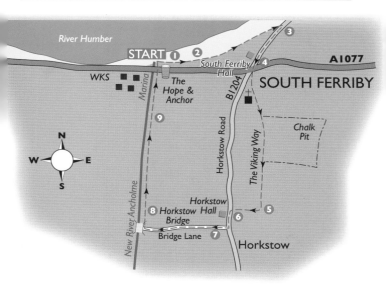

❺ After this last field by the telegraph poles, turn right, leaving the Viking Way, and walk down Horkstow Road. At the end of this road is a junction beside Hall Farm.

❻ Turn left at this junction and cross the road, using the footpath along the wall of Horkstow Hall. There are at least three Grade II listed 17th and 18th-century buildings in Horkstow. At the end of the pavement you reach Bridge Lane. Turn right here.

❼ Follow the peaceful Bridge Lane towards Horkstow Bridge. This Grade II listed suspension bridge was completed in 1836 as part of the River Ancholme drainage scheme. You do not cross this bridge, but bear right, taking the steps down to the path which follows the New River Ancholme.

South Ferriby Marina.

8 The hedge line should now be on your right as you follow the river for the next 1¼ miles.

9 You reach the last section when a number of moorings begin to appear and you come to a stile and metal gate. Continue ahead through the boatyard (South Ferriby Marina) until you re-join the footpath along the river. Pass through a gate by the yellow waymarker and walk towards the lock gates, which lead you back onto the pavement. Cross the road to the Hope and Anchor.

PLACES OF INTEREST NEARBY

The **Humber Bridge** is a great piece of civil engineering and links North Lincolnshire to Yorkshire. It was opened in 1981 having taken nine years to build. www.humberbridge.co.uk Directly beside the toll bridge exit on the East Riding and Hull side sits **Humber Bridge Country Park**, a 21-hectare, dog-friendly nature reserve with a bird feeding station and trails.

The peaceful trek across the fields.

2 Bradley Woods to Barnoldby le Beck

5 miles (8 km)

WALK HIGHLIGHTS

This makes a beautiful summer sunset walk. It crosses arable fields and woods in a peaceful setting with a welcome stop at an award-winning pub with a beer garden.

THE PUB

The Ship Inn, Barnoldby le Beck, **DN37 0BG**
Full of cosy charm the pub has a TripAdvisor Certificate of Excellence for serving some of the best food in the area.
☎ 01472 822308 www.the-shipinn.co.uk

THE WALK

1 From the Bradley Woods car park go through the metal gates and follow the road through the trees. When you reach the children's play area, turn left between two sets of swings and continue past the public bridleway sign.

Guide to Lincolnshire Pub Walks

HOW TO GET THERE AND PARKING: The walk starts at Bradley Woods on Bradley Road, just off the A46. As you enter the woods there is a small, free car park on the left. **Sat nav** DN37 0AL. If you choose to start your walk at the Ship Inn instead, begin at point 10. There is also a car park near the village church. **Sat nav** DN37 0BG.

MAP: OS Explorer 281 Ancholme Valley (GR TA 245058).

② Leave the woods through an opening in the trees, to enter arable farmland. Walk straight ahead with the hedge line on your left. At the end of this field, beside a copse, turn right.

③ Follow the hedge until you reach a junction at the end of the field. Bear right beside the lightning-destroyed tree and a yellow waymarker and follow a track between two arable fields. Walk between the pylons and continue ahead, crossing a wooden bridge.

④ Turn right and at the end of this field, turn left following the hedge on your left. Cross the road and continue ahead. After 100m, you reach the end of the field and leave via a gap in the hedge.

⑤ Turn left on to a bridleway which you follow round as it curves to the right and approaches Manor Top Farm. Pass a large green barn on your left and turn left, following the road, and begin to walk between two hedge lines.

⑥ Continue ahead with the Manor Golf Club on your right. As you follow the road, you will notice a solar farm on your left. Follow the public footpath sign ahead which sends you through the middle of the solar farm.

⑦ On leaving the solar farm there is a footpath ahead through an arable field towards a pylon. Should this be inaccessible because of crops, you can instead turn left and follow the field boundary round. At the end of the field, you meet a wooden bridge with a waymarker, bear left, passing the pylon towards the wood.

8 Reaching the end of this field, cross the track and enter the trees of Mount Pleasant West. Continue through the woods, crossing a junction with a clearing and remain ahead for the duration.

9 On leaving the woods, continue along a public footpath beside a farmhouse, where you follow the drive, passing a paddock on your right. At the end turn left onto the main road where you will see the Ship Inn ahead of you.

10 Just before the pub, turn left and walk down Chapel Lane, following the

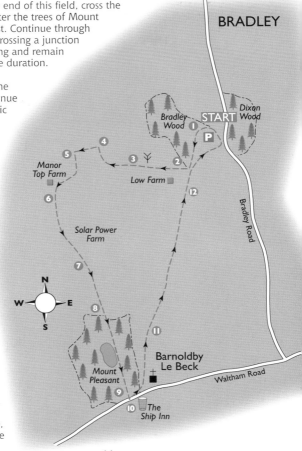

BRADLEY

Bradley Wood

Dixon Wood

START P

Manor Top Farm

Low Farm

Solar Power Farm

Bradley Road

N
W — E
S

Mount Pleasant

Barnoldby Le Beck

Waltham Road

The Ship Inn

'Wanderlust Way'. Continue on the road, bearing right and uphill, with the church on your left. At this point you will see another sign for 'The Wanderlust Way' and a sign stating '2 miles to Bradley Woods'.

11 You now continue to follow this track for the whole route back. You will notice Mount Pleasant West on your left. After a mile you reach a metal gate and a slight bend in the track. Continue ahead walking between two fields. At the end of this field you meet a metal gate where you turn right then immediately left, continuing along the field edge towards Bradley Woods. At the end of this field, the path forks. Bear right and continue towards the wood.

12 This field leads you back into Bradley Woods. Turn immediately right on entering and follow the path that skims the edge of the wood all the way back to the car park

PLACES OF INTEREST NEARBY

For typical seaside entertainment head 7 miles east to **Cleethorpes Seafront**. The pier and sandy beach for bathing belles is north of the town, with major entertainment complexes further south including the Pleasure Island theme park, the Discovery Centre and multiplex cinema. www.visitcleethorpes.co.uk.

Lincolnshire Wolds Railway, Ludborough, offers trips on a steam train through the Wolds. www.lincolnshirewoldsrailway.co.uk.

Wind turbines near point 2.

3 Tetney Lock
4.3 miles (7 km)

WALK HIGHLIGHTS

The first fascination for me on this route is walking through the Humberston Fitties, a pretty, painted chalet park. The second is the pond on the nature reserve, a popular place for children to go crabbing. This embankment walk takes in some distant views of the sea until you reach Louth Canal and follow the path down to the lockside pub. The route is suitable all year round, flat and simple to follow.

THE PUB

The Crown and Anchor, Tetney Lock, **DN36 5UW**
A friendly and welcoming pub that sits at the halfway point.
☎ 01472 388291   www.whatpub.com/pubs/LNE/NCT1/crown-anchor-tetney-lock

Guide to Lincolnshire Pub Walks

HOW TO GET THERE AND PARKING: This walk starts at a free RSPB car park. From the M180 take the A180 towards Grimsby and Cleethorpes. Once in Cleethorpes town centre follow the brown Holiday Park signs to Thorpe Park. At the park, continue to drive ahead past the roundabouts. You will see a car park on your left, but keep going. Continue to a one-way system with a sign for the Humberston Fitties chalet park, and continue ahead until you finally reach the end of the road, where there is a car park beside a lake and a yacht club. **Sat nav** DN36 4HE.

MAP: OS Explorer 283 Louth & Mablethorpe (GR TA 337050).

THE WALK

1 From the car park, walk along the track passing beside a nature pond. The chalets will be on your right as you head towards wind turbines. At the T-junction is a footpath sign, turn left here to walk along the sea defence embankment.

2 This path is a little under 2 miles long and heads towards the canal. Ignore the first footpath sign on your right. You'll then walk under a crude oil pipe and then to a small footbridge at the end of the path. Turn right here, following the Louth Canal.

3 After 600m you reach a gate with a waymarker. Pass through here and follow the canal to eventually reach a metal gate. Continue ahead.

4 The canal divides and you bear right. This leads to a bridge at the village of Tetney. Pass 'Coastguard Cottages' on your right as you turn left and walk over the bridge. Here you will see the Crown and Anchor pub.

5 On leaving the pub, cross the road and retrace your steps to the Coastguard Cottages. Turn right and follow the lane. At Newton Marsh Lane, turn left, walking away from the canal. This lane is just over a mile long and passes Braybrook Farm and eventually turns into a track. You reach a set of metal gates at the end of the track by a bend and a public footpath.

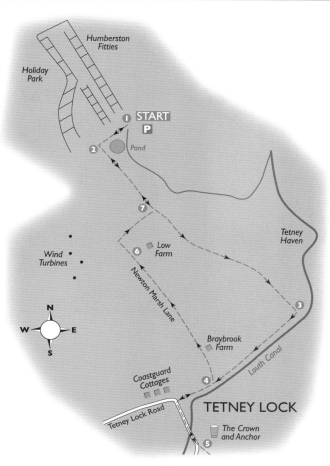

Humberston Fitties

Holiday Park

1 START
P

2 _Pond_

7

6 Low Farm

Wind Turbines

Newton Marsh Lane

Tetney Haven

3

Braybrook Farm

Louth Canal

Coastguard Cottages

4

Tetney Lock Road

TETNEY LOCK

The Crown and Anchor

5

N
W — E
S

15

6 Continue ahead down the side of the gates, where you will notice a wind farm on your left. After 100m, turn right at the T-junction by the waymarker and go ahead to a second waymarker on a bend at the edge of the field. Follow the path back towards the embankment, with the hedge line on your right.

Waltham Windmill.

7 At the end of this field you reach a wooden footbridge. Cross here and turn left onto the embankment. You now retrace your steps to the nature pond and the car park.

PLACES OF INTEREST NEARBY

Built in 1878 **Waltham Windmill** is a fully restored and working six-sailed windmill open to the public. The site has a pleasant rural atmosphere and has a coffee shop and restaurant. It is 6 miles from the Crown and Anchor. www.walthamwindmill.org.uk

Another popular attraction is **Cleethorpes Coast Light Railway**. This was established in 1948 and is one of Britain's oldest seaside miniature railways. It offers a 4-mile return journey along the Humberside coast www.cclr.co.uk Whilst here, you can enjoy a drink in the Signal Box Inn – the smallest pub on the planet!

Deer herd in the fields.

4 Tealby in the Wolds
4.6 miles (7.4 km)

WALK HIGHLIGHTS
Tealby is a quaint, striking village in the North Lincolnshire Wolds, an area famed for its beautiful hilly terrain. This walk along the Viking Way covers many fields grazed by livestock, including rare Lincoln Longwool sheep. Through fields of deer you climb until you reach a hilltop church, before easing back on a lower path along a country lane and footpaths.

THE PUB
The Kings Head, Tealby, **LN8 3YA**
An award-winning pub, said to be the oldest thatched pub in Lincolnshire, built around 1367. There is a large beer garden, a dining room and a cosy bar where dogs are welcome.
☎ 01673 838347   www.thekingsheadtealby.co.uk

THE WALK
1 From the Kings Head car park, turn left and cross the road, bearing right at the junction where the pavement disappears. Head in the direction of the church until you see a red telephone box on your left. Follow Church

Guide to Lincolnshire Pub Walks

HOW TO GET THERE AND PARKING: From Market Rasen, Tealby is 4 miles east on the B1203. The Kings Head lies at the far end of the village on Kingsway, a dead end. There is a large pub car park and off-road parking available in the village. **Sat nav** LN8 3YA.

MAP: OS Explorer 282, Lincolnshire Wolds North (GR TF 156904).

Lane, with the church on your right. This lane brings you to the main road at an information board. Turn left and after about 50m, cross the road towards the public footpath by a white building.

2 You are now on the Viking Way. Pass Field Cottage on your left and go towards a metal gate with a yellow waymarker into the field, continuing directly ahead on the trodden path. At the end of the field, go through the metal gate and follow the trodden path. Walk along the field edge, crossing some wooden boards. When you reach a public footpath sign, continue on this path, and do not turn off. At the next Viking Way sign, continue up the hill towards the wood.

3 As you reach the wood (Bedlam Plantation), you will see a derelict farm to your left (Castle Farm). Go through a gate into the wood, and skirt the edge of the plantation. After 100m you reach a metal gate where you continue ahead and then a second metal gate with a waymarker which takes you into a field. Walk diagonally across the field, passing another waymarker that leads you downhill and past a pond towards a series of gates at Risby Manor Farm. Follow the Viking Way and walk with the fence line on your right towards a bench and small souvenir 'Risby Flock' sheep hut with information board. Continue to the edge of the field where you meet a gate with a public footpath sign. Cross the track and follow the Viking Way.

4 Continue to walk with the fence on your right which takes you uphill past another waymarker where you continue to follow the path. Go over the rise and then back down the hill and through a metal gate, following the fence line on your right. This path leads uphill towards a copse marked with the Viking Way. Go through the opening, continuing to climb the hill and forge ahead at the next waymarker. Bear right towards the next marker.

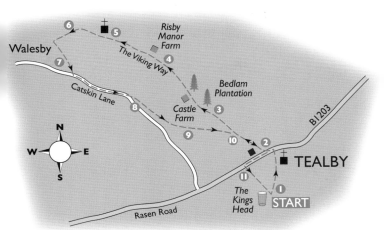

⑤ Go through the metal gate, crossing the track into the next field. Walk directly ahead towards the metal gate at the end of the field and in the next field, walk ahead with the fence line on your right, towards the church. Leave by the wooden gate into the church grounds where there is an information board. You can enter the church and explore the wild grounds.

⑥ Leave the churchyard through the wooden gate and follow the path downhill along a track, which can be muddy underfoot. The track becomes an access road, passes some houses and reaches a main road. Turn left onto Rasen Road and after 10m you will see a public footpath sign. To access this path, climb through a narrow access gap in the brick wall. The footpath skims beside some village gardens and leads you round to a metal gate into a field.

⑦ Continue along the path with the fence on your right towards the gate in the far bottom corner. Go through the gate and turn left onto Catskin Lane. Follow this quiet country lane for around ½ mile until you meet a bend in the road with a footpath sign on your left. Go through the hedges here, crossing a stile into a field.

8 Continue across the field with the fence on your right. Cross the next stile, go over a track and into the next field. You now cross this field towards the gate, following the waymarkers. Cross another field which you exit through a gate, then cross a small track and enter another field. Across this field is a gate and a small bridge into the next field. Follow the path across, with the fence on your left. From here you will see Castle Farm again. Go through the gate, across the track, and into the next field. Ensure the fence is on your right.

9 At the bottom of the field is an opening in the fence with a waymarker through a gate. Continue across the next field on the path towards the far right corner where there is a footpath sign, going through two gates to rejoin the Viking Way. Turn right.

10 With the hedge on your right, continue until you reach a gate and enter the next field. Continue to follow the hedge line, bearing uphill and passing a waymarker in the middle of the field. Continue up and across the field towards the village. At the end of this field, take the gate at the end, passing Field Cottage.

11 At the bottom of the track, turn right along the main road for 20m until you see a footpath on the left. Cross the road and follow the footpath leading down the side of some houses to a wooden gate into a field. Bear left on the field edge until you reach the end, leave by the gate and turn right. From here you can see the Kings Head.

PLACES OF INTEREST NEARBY

Market Rasen Racecourse is famed for its Boxing Day races. It holds a year-round programme of racing and also stages concerts.
www.marketrasen.thejockeyclub.co.uk

Brightwater Gardens are eight acres of beautiful gardens, wildflower meadows and woodland located at Saxby, 12 miles from Tealby.
www.brightwatergardens.co.uk

Tuetoes Wood at point 12.

5 Laughton Forest and Tuetoes Wood

7.2 miles (11.5 km)

WALK HIGHLIGHTS

This is an adventurous woodland walk leading into the pretty village of Laughton. There are many paths that weave through Laughton Forest, so ensure you have an OS map with you, or a map of the wood and its paths, available from www.forestry.gov.uk.

THE PUB

The Ingram Arms, Laughton, **DN21 3PR**
A friendly pub at the halfway point, with open fires in winter and a small beer garden.

☎ 01427 628465   www.ingramarms.co.uk

HOW TO GET THERE AND PARKING: Laughton Forest lies between Scunthorpe and Gainsborough, close to the River Trent. From Laughton, follow the East Ferry road, north of the village which takes you on a drive through the middle of the wood. Towards the end of this road you will see a sign for Laughton Forest on your right, leading into the free car park. **Sat nav** DN21 3JG.

MAP: OS Explorer 280 Isle of Axholme (GR SE 846010).

THE WALK

1 From the car park at Laughton Forest, take the main track which starts beside a barrier and follow it up towards the wood. At the first T-junction, turn right. In the summer, this particular section of path has an abundance of butterflies. At the next T-junction, turn right. Shortly afterwards, you meet a bend and a green barrier. Follow the path round to the left. This wide forest track leads you to a barrier at the end.

2 Walk around the barrier and continue ahead, crossing the main track through the wood. This section has no barrier, but does have a mound of earth blocking access for vehicles. The path takes you deeper into the woods for around ½ mile until you meet a T-junction at the end. Turn left and after 200m take the next right.

3 Follow this path for ½ mile, passing a farm and equestrian fields on your right formerly known as 'Jerry's Bog'. Continue ahead for another half a mile. The track leaves the wood and crosses a clearing to a country road.

4 Turn right here onto Scotter Road for just under ½ mile as it leads you into the village of Laughton. Pass a burial ground on your right and continue towards a bus stop on a road island. Here there is a signpost. Follow the direction of 'Blyton' and after 200m you will reach the Ingram Arms on the right.

5 On leaving the Ingram Arms, turn left and walk 200m back towards the signpost. Turn left, in the direction of 'East Ferry'. This leads you out of the village, passing a kindergarten on the first bend. Follow the village road until you reach the corner of Laughton Road at the junction. Bear right here, following the signs to 'East Ferry' which is marked as a cycle byway.

6 You now follow this quiet country road through the wood for around ½ mile. You cross a small bridge, marked with white posts either side and then further up pass a Border Collie rescue centre. Around 100m after the kennels, there is a turning on your right which you take.

7 This tree-lined road takes you back into the woods towards Laughton Bungalows and Laughton Cottages. There is a

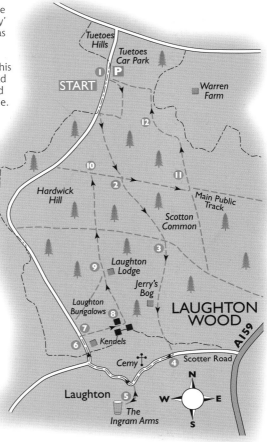

Tuetoes Hills

Tuetoes Car Park

1 START **P**

Warren Farm

12

10

2

11

Main Public Track

Hardwick Hill

Scotton Common

3

9

Laughton Lodge

Jerry's Bog

LAUGHTON WOOD

A159

Laughton Bungalows

8

7

6 Kennels

Cemy

4 Scotter Road

Laughton

5 The Ingram Arms

N
W E
S

slight incline up a track towards the end where there is an electricity pole and a barrier. Go around the barrier and bear left, under the yellow electricity poles.

8 You now walk deeper into the wood until you reach a single white house called 'Laughton Lodge' on your left. Follow the lodge's fence line which leads you further into the wood.

9 For the next mile, you continue ahead, ignoring any crossroads. You have reached the end of this section when you meet a metal barrier at the end of the track.

10 Turn right here, onto the main public track. The first turning you meet has a barrier on the left. (*If you wish to shorten your walk, you can take this path and retrace your steps from the start*.) Continue ahead for another ½ mile to explore the pretty Tuetoes Wood, where you meet a main crossroads with a metal barrier on your right. Turn left off the track here.

11 Follow this track back into the wood and turn left at the first junction, beside a ditch. You are now in Tuetoes Wood. After around 400m, you meet a clear path on your right which leads out of the wood into a clearing and towards the next section of woodland.

12 Continue to follow the clear woodland trail which eventually runs alongside a field with open views overlooking Warren Farm. At the first clear path on your left, turn in here and walk back into the wood. This eventually opens up as you walk beside reams of heather. When you reach the junction at the end, turn right, passing a small clear stream – ideal for dogs. Take the first left and follow the track towards the car park where you started.

PLACES OF INTEREST NEARBY

Less than 2 miles from Laughton is **Blyton Ice Cream Parlour**. It is a gem of a find serving over 60 different flavours of ice cream. Hot food, snacks and cakes are also available in their indoor and outdoor café. You can find it on the High Street in Blyton, DN21 3LA, or check out its opening hours on their website www.blytonicecream.co.uk.

Crab Tree Walk Plantation at point 8.

6 Little Cawthorpe
7.2 miles (11.5 km)

WALK HIGHLIGHTS
This walk is a great ramble through the countryside, past woods, across cornfields and down peaceful single-track lanes, some of which are through the hamlet of Little Cawthorpe alongside pretty cottages. The final stroll along the water's edge to a ford is a delight, especially when there is a lovely country pub beside it in tranquil grounds. To fully appreciate this walk, I suggest doing it in spring or summer, before the arable fields are ploughed and left plain to the eye and muddy underfoot.

THE PUB
The Royal Oak Inn, Little Cawthorpe, **LN11 8LZ**
Known as 'The Splash' and dating from the 17th century, this cosy pub offers great food and real ale.
☎ 01507 600750 www.royaloaksplash.co.uk

Guide to Lincolnshire Pub Walks

HOW TO GET THERE AND PARKING: From the A16, near Louth, join the A157 and follow this until you see signs for Little Cawthorpe. Turn off and park on Watery Lane or at the Royal Oak, if you are dining there. **Sat nav** LN11 8LZ.

MAP: OS Explorer 282 Lincolnshire Wolds North (GR TF 358838).

THE WALK

1 From the Royal Oak, turn left and walk towards a footpath sign and follow Coggles Way. After 50m, cross a bridge over a stream, following the waymarker. This path leads round to a wooded area, before meeting a white gate at the end. Turn left onto the lane.

2 Immediately turn right onto Haugham Pastures and walk along this quiet lane for $1/3$ mile. After passing a wood yard, continue for another 200m until you reach a bridleway sign where you turn left.

3 Follow the farm track, ignoring the first waymarker on your left. Enjoy the rising views around you as your path eventually bends round towards a solitary oak tree with a waymarker nailed to the trunk.

4 Here, turn right and walk between two fields up to the edge of Haugham Woods. Turn right and follow the path that runs alongside the wood and steadily climbs uphill. After $1/2$ mile, look out for a clear opening into the wood. This narrow and well-trodden path skims along the wood edge and leads you down a steep section towards a stile. There is a yellow waymarker bearing left.

5 Climb uphill towards the next stile. Cross the field towards a waymarker and continue ahead, following the edge of the woods.

6 At the end of the wood you reach a footpath sign, follow this ahead between two fields towards a solitary tree at the end by another footpath sign. Now follow the path ahead through the next field.

7 At the end is another sign. Turn right and follow this track. You reach two metal cylinders at the next sign. Turn left here.

3 This track runs for a mile, passing fields and with views towards Burwell. At the footpath sign, turn left towards Crab Tree Walk Plantation. At the edge of the wood, follow the waymarked path between two fields and head towards Burwell Wood.

9 On reaching Burwell Wood, you reach a footpath sign by an opening in the hedge. Take this path, which can be muddy underfoot, down some steps. Wade across the wood until you climb back uphill to a public footpath sign.

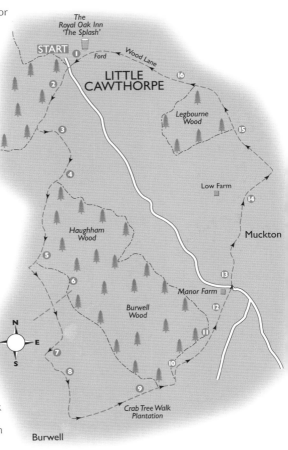

27

10 Turn left here, then immediately right, following the edge of Burwell Wood. At the end, continue across the track towards a gate. Continue ahead.

11 When you reach the end of this wood, you'll see a footpath sign. Continue ahead across the field towards the trees. At the other end is a gap in the hedge which you go through, passing overgrowth to reach a stile. Any dogs should be on a lead here as the field beyond the stile usually contains livestock.

12 Turn right into this field, following the field edge towards the stile at the end beside the house. Here there is a waymarker leading you across Manor Farm, past the farmhouse and barn, towards a road junction.

13 Turn left onto the road, and follow it until you see a sharp bend and a sign for Holcroft Cottage. Turn right to follow the bridleway up a single-track lane. Follow this quiet lane for around a mile until it turns into a junction near Low Farm. At a waymarker bear right and follow the track to the end of the field beside a dismantled railway.

14 Beside the fence, is a bridleway sign. Turn left and follow the field edge towards Legbourne Wood.

15 This path leads you into the wood by a waymarker. A bridleway sign appears and you remain ahead. You reach a sign for Legbourne Wood. Continue ahead until you leave the wood and meet a lane.

16 Stay on this lane which eventually takes you down Wood Lane into Little Cawthorpe. After a few houses, continue ahead towards the ford. Use the footbridge and walk along this pleasant water-side path. At the end is the ford where you cross the footbridge onto Watery Lane and continue to the Royal Oak on your left.

PLACES OF INTEREST NEARBY

Hubbard's Hills is a beautiful park in Louth. It has a riverside path, open hills and a cliff ridge, and there is a small café.

The motor racing circuit at **Cadwell Park** is reputed to be one of the best circuits in the country favoured for motorbike racing. For a full fixtures list www.cadwellpark.co.uk.

The Fossdyke Navigation.

7 Lincoln City and the Waterfront

5 miles (8 km)

WALK HIGHLIGHTS

A city walk is not often regarded as the first choice by walkers. However, this all-season route begins with a country pub and a waterfront stroll along England's oldest canal, thought to have been built by the Romans in AD 120. You then continue to the cultural quarter to view the delights of Lincoln Cathedral and Lincoln Castle, before climbing back down the infamous Steep Hill. This in turn leads you the vibrant Brayford Waterfront, where there are many places to enjoy some street café life.

THE PUB

The Pyewipe Inn, Saxilby Road, **LN1 2BG**
Sitting on the oldest man-made waterway, the Fossdyke Navigation, there is plenty of outside space to enjoy the waterfront views.
☎ 01522 528708 www.pyewipe.co.uk

Guide to Lincolnshire Pub Walks

HOW TO GET THERE AND PARKING: The Pyewipe Inn car park is beside the A46 between Skellingthorpe and Burton where it crosses the canal. On the A57 Saxilby Road, just north of the A46, there is a large roadside sign for the pub which leads down a long single-track lane. There is a charge of £1 for non-patrons. **Sat nav** LN1 2BG.

MAP: OS Explorer 272 Lincoln (GR SK 948723).

THE WALK

1 From the Pyewipe Inn, take the canal path towards the city centre for a mile. The canal should be on your right.

2 After passing the Carholme Golf Club you meet a public footpath sign. Turn left here and walk along the edge of the golf club, following the waymarkers. You exit through a gap in the hedge beside traffic lights. Cross this road and continue ahead, following the footpath sign through two sets of metal gates. Where the path forks, bear right and head uphill on Alderman's Walk.

3 Leave Alderman's Walk by a gate at the top and turn right, walking towards the pedestrian crossing on Yarborough Road. Once over, turn left and head to the corner of Upper Long Leys Road. Turn up here and begin a short steep climb.

4 Immediately after Willis Close on your right, take the footpath beside the last terraced house. Follow this as it bears left and comes out onto Westgate. Turn right, and right again as you follow Union Road towards Lincoln Castle.

5 The west entrance to the castle emerges after the Victoria pub. Walk up the bridge into the castle grounds. *You do not have to pay to use this as a walk through, only if you wish to take a tour.* Follow this path around the castle and the Crown Court, and head towards the gateway at the end. You will have a clear view of Lincoln Cathedral from here.

6 On passing through the castle gateway, you enter the cultural quarter and will see the Magna Carter pub. Turn right and begin the walk downhill.

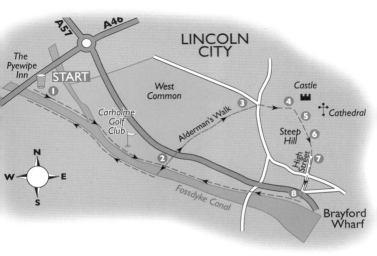

You pass many tearooms and pubs on this section, including Browns Pie Shop. When you reach the cosy Bookstop Café, the road forks and you bear left down Steep Hill where there are many interesting shops.

7 Steep Hill gradually merges into the High Street, bringing you back to the 21st century. Continue to walk down the High Street and under the clock tower, where after 100m you reach a large black and white Tudor building on your right, Stokes High Bridge Café, which offers good food and fabulous views. On your immediate right beside the café is an opening which you go through and walk along the River Witham (the river on your left). Follow this path round and under a bridge where you will see the Odeon cinema ahead.

8 You now enter Brayford Wharf and pass the Royal William IV pub. Continue to follow this path along the Fossdyke Navigation, passing

The Pyewipe Inn.

Lincoln University across the water on your left. Now follow this path for the next 2 miles all the way back to the Pyewipe Inn.

PLACES OF INTEREST NEARBY

Begun in 1088, **Lincoln Cathedral** is the third largest cathedral in the country. This majestic architectural masterpiece is open for tours and there is an admission charge. Alternatively, **Brayford Belle Boat Trips** run one-hour excursions. You can also use the water taxi for return travel to the Pyewipe Inn. www.lincolnboattrips.co.uk.

The nature reserve at Snipe Dales.

8 Snipe Dales Round to Hagworthingham

6 miles (9.5 km)

WALK HIGHLIGHTS

This is a very attractive walk, which can be hilly in sections. Explore Snipe Dales, one of the most stunning country parks in Lincolnshire, and the pretty village of Hagworthingham, strewn with cottages. Please note that dogs are not allowed in the Snipe Dales nature reserve, but they are welcome in the country park.

THE PUB

The George & Dragon, Hagworthingham, **PE23 4NA**
Offers good food and a friendly welcome.
☎ 01507 588255 www.facebook.com/georgendragonpub

THE WALK

1 From the Snipe Dales car park, walk towards the red brick building and turn left, following the red waymarker which leads you downhill to cross a wooden footbridge. Continue ahead up a steep hill and along the top for 50m until you reach the nature reserve on your left.

Guide to Lincolnshire Pub Walks

HOW TO GET THERE AND PARKING: Snipe Dales Country Park is near Lusby between Horncastle and Spilsby off the B1195. It is well signposted from the A158 and B1195. Parking is available for a small daily charge. **Sat nav** PE23 4JB.

MAP: OS Explorer 273 Lincolnshire Wolds South (GR TF 331682).

2 Follow the path downhill to the nature reserve until you reach a wooden gate on your left. Continue through the gate and along the hilly terrain until you reach a red waymarker. Turn right, gradually heading downhill and cross the wooden footbridge, where you turn right. At the next gate turn left, following the path uphill and go through another wooden gate passing Clark's Wood. You will see another waymarker as you begin to descend towards a wooden footpath sign.

3 Turn left at the 'footpath to Hagworthingham' sign. Follow this path down towards a wooden bridge, cross, and follow the yellow waymarker ahead. There is a fence on your right as you begin to ascend along the field edge. You will see another waymarker which takes you through an enclosure of trees. This trail heading uphill can be overgrown and muddy underfoot at times. Leave through the gate at the end.

4 You now walk between two fields uphill and continue as the path bears right towards hedges. There is a public footpath sign at an opening in the hedge.

5 Bear left, heading downhill towards a track. Follow this track for 1/3 mile until you reach a sharp left turn by a waymarker. Continue ahead for 1/2 mile along a green bank that runs between two fields.

6 At the end climb over the stile in the hedgerow and follow the narrow path towards another gate. Continue ahead, passing a large green barn and leave by the wooden gate with the yellow marker. This path runs between two gardens towards the road at the end.

7 Turn left into the village. There are no footpaths through this area of Hagworthingham, so take care. When you reach Holy Trinity Church, go

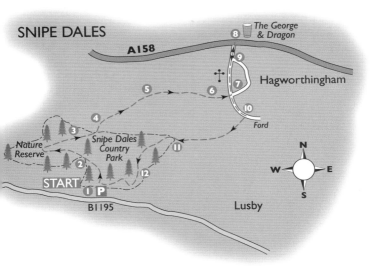

through the gate, walking along the edge of the churchyard and out of the gate the other end. *This section of road is very narrow but is the safest option for pedestrians.* Continue to take care as you walk through the village, passing the many road-side cottages.

⑧ At the top of the road, you meet a junction before the A158. Turn right, following the sign for Sausthorpe & Skegness. This brings you out to JJ's Café and further along, you will see the George & Dragon. Take care when crossing the busy A158.

⑨ From the pub, cross the road and turn right. Take the first left into Hagworthingham, retracing your steps down Church Lane through the village. Take the path through the churchyard again and continue out of the village until you reach a large white gate on your right. Here you meet a ford.

10 Cross the wooden footbridge over the ford and turn immediately right towards the footpath for Snipe Dales. Follow this footpath through Beckside Meadow for the next ¾ mile that follows the stream and takes you through a wooden gate.

Gunby Hall.

11 You reach Snipe Dales beside a babbling brook. On entering, bear left at the first junction and you will see a red waymarker. Continue to follow this path alongside a stream for around ½ mile until you reach a crossroads. Turn left.

12 Cross a small bridge and continue to bear left as the path gradually climbs uphill. At the top, turn right at the wooden barrier by the red waymarker into an enclosure of trees. On leaving this wooded area, head down a steep path, turning left at the junction and left again towards the red waymarker. The final stretch of path descends and then climbs once more, before finally going down through an enclosure of trees towards a sign for the car park.

PLACES OF INTEREST NEARBY

The small, pretty town of **Horncastle** is full of antique shops and is home to the Sir Joseph Banks Centre. Banks was a British naturalist, botanist and patron of the natural sciences in the 18th century, famous for his expedition with Captain Cook. In the opposite direction is **Gunby Estate, Hall and Gardens** owned by the National Trust. Here you will find Victorian walled gardens and a house dating back to 1700. www.nationaltrust.org.uk/gunby-estate-hall-and-gardens.

Alternatively The **Walled Garden Baumber**, is also thoroughly worth a visit. Walk around the 19th-century four acre garden that once belonged to Stourton Hall, before a well-earned stop in the tearoom. www.walledgardenbaumber.co.uk

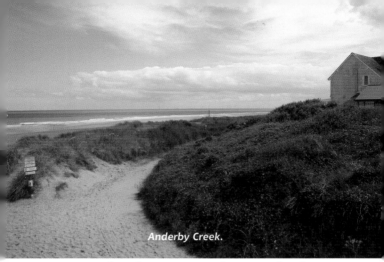
Anderby Creek.

9 Anderby Creek and the Great Coastal Escape

5.6 miles (9 km)

WALK HIGHLIGHTS

The Lincolnshire coast is most famous for Skegness, 'the Blackpool of the east', however, the Wash also hides many beautiful stretches of quiet, long golden beaches that only the locals know of. Anderby Creek is such a place and is particularly popular with dog walkers out of season. It's easy to see why. The walk takes you down quiet lanes and good footpaths alongside arable fields and ends with a scenic trek through the dunes.

THE PUB

Popa's Bar, Anderby Creek, **PE24 5XW**
Only 200m from the beach and serves good local seasonal food.
☎ 01754 873752 www.popasbar.co.uk

Guide to Lincolnshire Pub Walks

HOW TO GET THERE AND PARKING: Take the A52 towards Alford and Chapel St Leonards then follow the signs to Anderby Creek on a pretty coastal road north. There is a free beach car park. **Sat nav** PE24 5XX.

MAP: OS Explorer 274, Skegness, Alford & Spilsby (GR TF 552762).

THE WALK

1 From the car park turn left as you face Popa's Bar. Walk towards the beach and up the sandy bank towards the 'Cloud Bar' then down towards the sea and turn right. Beware of being cut off by pockets of water if you walk close to the sea.

2 Follow the beach for 2 miles. Pass Wolla Bank and Chapel Six Marshes, marked by a blue sculpture. Turn right at Chapel Point, which is clearly marked by the North Sea Observatory (open to the public).

3 Pass the Point Café and cross the main road towards the houses in the direction of Eastfields Park. Chapel Point Nature Area is on your left. As you reach Eastfields Park, turn right towards the barriers, following the public footpath sign.

4 Once inside the caravan park, walk ahead along the main road for around 200m, turning left at the next footpath sign. After another 20m, there is another footpath sign directing you across the grassed area. Turn right at the waymarker and head towards the wooden footbridge. Cross this and bear left, walking alongside the stream towards a waymarker, directing you right. Now walk on a path between two fences leading to a gate at the end into Nelson Villa.

5 Continue ahead, passing the house on your right as you leave the caravan park onto Maiden Lane. Follow the lane ahead until you come to a T-junction. Bear right and continue along the lane until you reach Stones Lane, the first turning on your right, beside a signpost for Anderby Creek.

6 Follow this lane for ½ mile, passing arable farms, before reaching a house on a huge plot called 'Mole End'. Continue to follow the footpath ahead which circumvents the property. This path leads you between two fields towards a T-junction at the end.

7 Turn right for Anderby Creek and follow this path as it curves round towards a metal gate and another footpath sign. Turn right here, following the sign for 'Roman Bank'. Continue along Ember Lane and pass Bank Farm at the end.

8 At the road junction, turn left, taking care on this short section. You will pass a large pond on your left and head towards the junction on the bend. Here, take care when turning right into Wolla Bank. Follow the road for 100m until you reach the car park.

9 Walk to the end of the car park to the footpath sign and take this path for ¾ mile which directs you towards the bird hide.

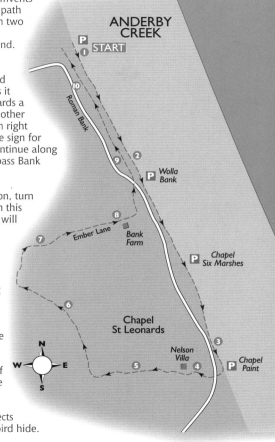

39

Seafront houses at point 10.

10 At the junction for the bird hide, turn right, following the path round by the waymakers. Take the steps and walk down the boardwalk. Take the immediate left turn at the bottom and walk along the dunes towards the seafront houses. At the crossroads, turn left, then right onto the path beside the houses. At the end of this path, turn left, back down the sandy path and into the car park.

PLACES OF INTEREST NEARBY

Never underestimate the power of Skeggy! **Skegness** rakes in thousands of day-trippers and holiday makers every year with its abundance of arcades, fairground attractions, sandy beaches and kiss-me-quick hats. There are chip shops, cafés and seafood stalls everywhere and it's only 10 miles south of Anderby Creek. Everyone should visit at least once in their life-time! If you like tearooms more than chip shops you may prefer the coastal village of **Sutton-on-Sea**, just 5 miles north. It is known for its award-winning sandy beaches, well-kept seafront gardens and traditional family attractions.

Tattershall Castle.

10 Tattershall Thorpe and the River Bain

5.5 miles (8.8 km)

WALK HIGHLIGHTS

If you can, allow plenty of time to see some lovely attractions on this route. You'll stroll through woods where there are old bomb shelters, pass Thorpe Camp Visitor Centre and explore the banks of the River Bain. Worth a closer look is Holy Trinity Church, with its beautiful stained-glass windows and Tattershall Castle next door, where you can climb up the tower to view the beautiful Lincolnshire countryside. You will see aircraft exhibits as you pass the Battle of Britain Memorial Flight Visitor Centre, and as you head back through Coningsby there are plenty of cafés if you are in need of refreshment.

THE PUB

The Blue Bell Inn, Tattershall Thorpe **LN4 4PE**
Built in 1257, this stunning cottage-style pub has the beams and open fires you would expect. It serves good food and over the years has been the haunt of Royalist Fugitives and RAF heroes including the 'Dambusters' Squadron.
☎ 01526 342206 www.bluebell-inn.com

Guide to Lincolnshire Pub Walks

HOW TO GET THERE AND PARKING: There is a public car park in Coningsby with ample spaces and public toilets. From the A153 east coast road towards Coningsby turn off by the church signposted 'Battle of Britain Memorial Flight'. The car park is first on the left behind the shops. **Sat nav** LN4 4SG.

MAP: OS Explorer 261 Boston (GR TF 224580).

THE WALK

1 From the car park, head out towards the main road (A153). You will see the church clock on your left. Cross over the A153 at the pedestrian crossing and turn right. After 100m, you will see a public footpath sign on Mason's Lane beside the Black Swan pub. Turn left here and continue ahead along a footpath over the river. This brings you to a lane where you continue directly ahead over a stile following the public footpath. There is a large gap in the hedge suitable for bigger dogs to get through.

2 Follow the fieldside path ahead until you meet a group of trees and a yellow waymarker. Ascend over a disused railway and into a field, continuing ahead until you reach a minor road. Turn right here and walk towards Tattershall Thorpe.

3 When you reach the road junction, turn left and cross the road, walking through the village. Here you will see the Blue Bell Inn. As you leave the village, you will see Thorpe Camp Visitor Centre on the left (this has limited opening hours, but is worth a visit). Cross the road towards the entrance, where there is a gap in the fence on your left. Go through this and follow the path towards the gate ahead.

4 At the gate, turn right into the Woodland Trust's Tattershall Thorpe Carr. *This wood is famed for being part of RAF Woodhall Spa during the Second World War, home of the 617 Dambuster Squadron. Through these woods you will see several old bomb shelters, which now house bats, and in spring there is a spectacular display of bluebells.* After 20m, cross the footbridge and continue to follow the path along the edge of the woods, which can be muddy underfoot in wet weather. Ignore any other paths on your left. When you reach the edge of the woods, your path will bear left and this is where you will see the old bomb shelters. On approaching two shelters close together, turn right on the path and head towards the gate.

5 You now venture out into open countryside, walking between two hedges. When you come to the next footpath sign, continue ahead towards the wood, marked at the end by a gate. Enter Tattershall Carr, cross a footbridge and turn left. Continue to follow this path, ignoring paths on the right (they can be used but tend to be more muddy underfoot). Again, you will pass old bomb shelters through here and at the end of the wood you reach a minor road.

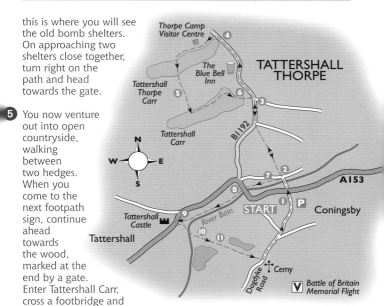

6 Turn right and follow the road round as you leave Tattershall Thorpe and pass Carrwood Crescent. After 100m, you reach the same footpath sign used earlier. Turn left here into the field and follow this route back, which goes over the disused railway and towards the stile onto the lane.

7 After 50m, you come to a bridge. Turn right, following the footpath sign by the gate and walk along the banks of the River Bain towards the church.

Guide to Lincolnshire Pub Walks

8 After ½ mile, you reach a road bridge. Leave through the gate, turn left and cross the road with care. You will see another footpath sign that continues to follow the river bank and you will now start to get views of Tattershall Castle and Holy Trinity Church.

9 After 800m you reach a bridge over a weir. Follow the path over the bridge, passing a wooden footbridge on your right. Immediately afterwards is a lane on your left which is not marked. Follow this lane, passing a car park as you reach Holy Trinity Church. *It is worth spending an hour or so here to view this majestic building.*

10 Once you have finished at the church and castle, retrace your steps down the lane and past the car park and turn right towards the bridge over the weir. Cross the bridge and turn right. Continue to follow the river bank for 30m, where you will see a track on your left, marked by a yellow waymarker.

11 Follow this path for about ½ mile. Remember to look back and enjoy the beautiful views of the church and castle behind you. You will pass some fishing lakes on your way back towards Coningsby. At the end you reach a metal gate and stile and continue ahead towards the road. There is a cemetery opposite. Turn left and walk through Coningsby to a mini roundabout. If you are still peckish, there is the Ginger Cow Coffee House on your left. Continue ahead past the chip shop and the car park entrance is 50m on your left.

PLACES OF INTEREST NEARBY

Tattershall Castle has its origins as far back as 1231 and is one of the earliest and finest surviving examples of English medieval brickwork. **Holy Trinity Church** is just next door, built around 1466. Both were built by Lord Ralph Cromwell, Treasurer of England. Plane enthusiasts should head to the **Battle of Britain Memorial Flight Visitor Centre** where you can have guided tours of the hanger and view the famous aircraft. Alternatively visit **Woodhall Spa**, an extremely stylish 1920s 'village' with manicured grounds in Jubilee Park, the famous Kinema in the Woods, and tearooms and cafés in abundance.

Farmland surrounding Stapleford Woods.

11 Norton Disney to Stapleford Woods

5.5 miles (8.8 km)

WALK HIGHLIGHTS

This lovely walk takes in the tranquil pretty villages of Stapleford and Norton Disney, as well as Stapleford Woods, Stapleford Moor and beautiful tracks that run alongside it. The route offers a variety of scenery and will be most enjoyed during spring and summer when the ground is hard underfoot.

THE PUB

The Green Man, Norton Disney, **LN6 9JU**
A traditional pub and restaurant with a large beer garden.
☎ 01522 789804   www.thegreenman-nortondisney.co.uk

Guide to Lincolnshire Pub Walks

HOW TO GET THERE AND PARKING: The Green Man is just off the A17 or can be reached via the A46 and is 7 miles east of Newark. There is a car park for patrons or off-road parking beside pub. **Sat nav** LN6 9JU.

MAP: OS Explorer 271 Newark-on-Trent (GR SK 888591).

THE WALK

1 From the Green Man car park, walk through the beer garden following the public footpath sign. Go through the gate at the end of the beer garden and turn left, following the hedge all the way around the edge of the field until you reach a metal gate with a small wooden bridge. From here turn left, following the footpath which heads towards Stapleford.

2 Follow this footpath, bearing right along the fence line for 1 mile. This area can become very damp underfoot in winter. You reach the end of this section when you meet a gate to your right. Turn left towards the village sign for Stapleford. You will walk on the road for a short distance and then take the path through the village.

3 Follow the village path, bearing right round a bend and continue along the High Street and passing Hunts Farm. Leave Stapleford along Newark Road. As you reach a tight bend in the road, cross over where there is a public footpath sign onto Moor Lane.

4 Continue along Moor Lane for ¾ mile until you reach the first public footpath sign beside Moor Farm. Turn right onto Lodge Drive (not signposted) which takes you into the woods.

5 Follow Lodge Drive through the woods and continue ahead until you reach Coddington Lane. From here, turn right onto the road until you reach a triangular junction with a large horse chestnut tree on it. Bear left towards the 'Give Way' sign and then after 10m, turn right at the footpath sign onto Stapleford Moor.

6 Follow the bridleway through the moor. This can be muddy underfoot during winter. You come out of the woods into a clearing and continue

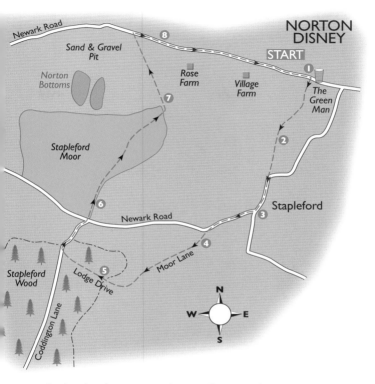

to walk ahead. When you reach a small crossroads, continue ahead following the arrow. The clearing ends and you bear right, then bear immediately left into the woods, following the arrows.

7 At the end of this woodland path, you reach a bridleway sign. Turn left and cross a small wooden bridge. As you continue along this path, you

Stapleford Woods.

will see Norton Bottoms on your left and also a quarry in the distance. You will need to cross the quarry track as you continue along this country path until you reach a road at the end.

8 Turn right onto the quiet Newark Road and walk for just over a mile, passing Rose Farm and Village Farm, back to the Green Man at Norton Disney.

PLACES OF INTEREST NEARBY

In the town centre stands the ruined **Newark Castle** which was besieged by Parliamentary forces during the Civil War. The **National Civil War Centre** is the newest addition to complement the town's rich history. www.nationalcivilwarcentre.com.

Beautiful fields overlook the Vales.

12 Barkston and the Trainspotter's Delight

6.5 miles (10.4 km)

WALK HIGHLIGHTS

This walk is a trainspotter's delight with both the fast north-south intercity and the steady east-west coastal train crossing your path. Enjoy the peaceful rambling hillsides, the pretty village of Marston and, towards the end of the walk, a welcoming stroll along the River Witham. You'll cross mainly arable fields, which make it more picturesque in spring and summer.

THE PUB

The Stag, Barkston **NG32 2NB**

This traditional country pub, with plenty of charm, wooden beams, an open fire and award-winning ales, offers bar food and a restaurant menu prepared by an award-winning chef. There is a beer garden and the pub is dog friendly.

☎ 01400 250363 www.thestagbarkston.co.uk

THE WALK

1 From the Stag, cross over the A607, bearing right (there is an island

Guide to Lincolnshire Pub Walks

HOW TO GET THERE AND PARKING: The Stag is on the A607 at Barkston, 4 miles north of Grantham. It sits on the main road, beside a green. The Stag has limited parking but off-road parking is available nearby. **Sat nav** NG32 2NB.

MAP: OS Explorer 247 Grantham (GR SK 931415).

further along for crossing near the telephone box) and head towards West Street. Continue to walk down this street past cottages until you reach the last house. On your right there is a telegraph pole and a public footpath sign leading you into a field.

2 Cross the field diagonally until you reach the waymarker at the end, between two trees. Continue into the next arable field, crossing a small bridge. Walk diagonally across this field and when you reach the hedge line, continue into the next field, bearing right to a bridleway sign. Continue to follow this track. This path takes you under the railway bridge on Drift Lane, where you continue ahead.

3 After crossing a small stone bridge, there is a bridleway sign. Turn left. After 100m, there is another signpost where the track forks. Take the higher road, bearing uphill which is part of the Viking Way. As the path curves round to the left, you reach a T-junction overlooking Old Gorse Wood. Bear right at this junction, continuing along the track.

4 At Frinkley Lane, there is a restricted byway sign. Turn left, towards the wind turbine and leave the Viking Way. Continue along this path, which can be overgrown in sections, making it unsuitable in winter, and continue towards Frinkley Farm.

5 After passing through Frinkley Farm, turn left, following the hedge towards the railway. There is no public footpath sign visible, but ensure you take this grassy path before you reach the red brick house on your left. It brings you down into Marston.

6 Leaving Frinkley Lane, turn left beside the Hougham and Marston village hall. Follow the path into Marston, crossing the bridge over the River

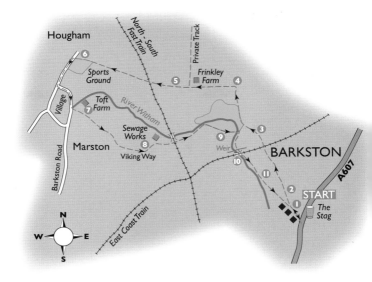

Witham. You will see the church of St Mary on your left and also the Thorold Arms pub. At the time of going to press, the Thorold Arms was not in operation and the village community was trying buy it (www. save.thethoroldarms.co.uk). At the pub, turn left into School Lane and re-join the Viking Way. You will pass the Victorian school of Marston and Thorold, built in 1861, on your right. This path then curves to the right onto Barkston Road. The last house you reach is called The Hollies, where you turn left down a no through road, marked for the Viking Way.

7 You are now on Hougham Mill Lane, passing Toft Farm on your left. Follow the bridleway until you reach the end beside a private road. Continue ahead along the bridleway, beside the high fence. Follow this path to the end beside another sign and turn left onto the Viking Way. Follow this path by a series of large metal barrels until you reach the end.

8 Turn left, following the road beside the sewage works. To the right of the sewage works gates is a bridleway. Take this path which runs alongside it on the Viking Way, bearing left where it forks. Go under the railway bridge, following the trail along the field edge and then beside the River Witham. This is a good section for trainspotting and the *Flying Scotsman* can sometimes be seen on the north-south line.

9 At the end of this section of river is Mickling Plantation, marked by a bridleway sign. Turn right here, then after 100m, left, following the path through the field. At the end of the field you come to a large metal bridge. Turn right and follow the river. Cross the river where the weir is shown on the map. This is not well marked and can be overgrown, although if you have a dog they will find it straight away! The route curves inwards, towards a small overgrown path (if you reach the railway bridge, you have gone too far). Here there are large stepping stones to cross the weir, although it is not advisable to use these after heavy rainfall.

10 Once over the river, you enter a small wooded area beside a waymarker. If you have one, put your dog on a lead now as immediately after this is a pedestrian railway crossing. Take care when crossing the track. This is the Skegness to Nottingham line and is not used by high speed trains. You then head straight into a livestock field on the other side. Bear left through the field, leaving by a metal gate at the end.

11 Continue ahead along the bridleway, passing Mill Farm which is also a Caravan Club site. At the next signpost, continue down the track towards Barkston village. You now begin to retrace your steps past the cottages along West Street. At the end, cross the A607 again towards The Stag.

PLACES OF INTEREST NEARBY

Belton House is one of the National Trust's most treasured possessions and is only two miles west of The Stag on the A607. The Grade I listed house was built in 1685 and sits in stunning formal gardens with woodland, a lake and acres of deer park. www.nationaltrust.org.uk/belton-house. A favourite in the summer is **Syston Fruit Farm**. The pick-your-own fruits entice many to this hill top retreat. It has a farm shop and café with outdoor seating so you can enjoy the expansive views. www.systonparkfarmshop.com.

The lock at Woolsthorpe by the Dirty Duck pub.

13 Grantham Canal and the Vale of Belvoir

7 miles (11 km)

WALK HIGHLIGHTS

This walk is a great introduction to 'The Vales' with its stone cottage villages and beautiful countryside. It begins along the Grantham Canal before climbing the Viking Way and following a path down to the village of Denton where you will explore Denton Reservoir, with its abundant birdlife.

THE PUB

The Dirty Duck, Woolsthorpe, **NG32 1NY**
A lovely canalside pub with plenty of outdoor seating and excellent food.
☎ 01476 870111 www.thedirtyduckpub.co.uk

Guide to Lincolnshire Pub Walks

HOW TO GET THERE AND PARKING: From the A52, turn off at the Bottesford bypass on to Belvoir Road, following signs for Woolsthorpe. Turn left onto Woolsthorpe Road and follow this until you reach a crossroads at Woolsthorpe. Turn left, then right when you see the sign for the Dirty Duck. **Sat nav** NG32 1NY.

MAP: OS Explorer 247 Grantham (GR SK 843352).

THE WALK

1 From the Dirty Duck car park, turn left and cross the bridge over the canal. Turn immediately right and go through the gate that takes you along the canal towards Woolsthorpe Lock (No.17). Continue along this path for ½ mile until you reach bridge No.62. Turn left by the bridge, going through the metal gate and cross the bridge.

2 There is a bridleway sign and a Viking Way sign. Follow the Viking Way for the next 2 miles, firstly climbing up the vales along a shady path. You will come across sections of dismantled railway and their disused bridges. Half way through this section, take care crossing Cliff Road by the gate to Belvoir Castle. Over the road bear left to pick up the Viking Way ahead beside the trees. You approach the end of this section when you meet a clearing beside a field. Continue ahead, over a disused railway bridge and walk for a further 20m.

3 On your right you will see cottages, and on your left is a blue National Cycle Network sign. Turn left here, following the cycle route, with the trees and hedge on your left. Pass Denton Manor Farm after ½ mile. Bear left here, then immediately right, as you continue to follow the cycle path. Further ahead is a large brick bridge. Go under the bridge and turn immediately right, to re-pass through the upper arch and follow the path up to Belvoir Road.

4 Turn right and follow this country road for ½ mile as it heads into the village of Denton. When you reach the village, stay on the main path as it bears left until you reach Casthorpe Road by the signpost for 'Denton Wharf'. Turn left and continue along the road for around 100m until you see a public footpath sign on your right. Turn right.

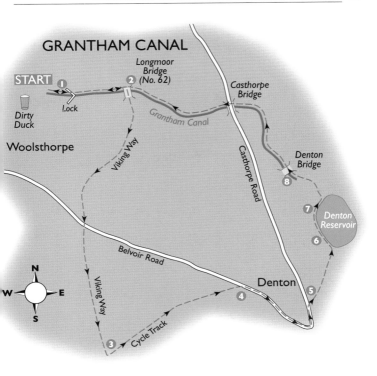

5 This section begins along a clear stream, perfect for dogs. Continue ahead, passing through a metal gate with a waymarker. Continue ahead, with a fence line on your right. There is a white gate and a stile at the end of this field.

6 You will now walk along Denton Reservoir in a clockwise direction. Halfway round the reservoir you see an obvious sloping path emerging

from your left. Bear left here, walking down the slope towards a small stream and a sign welcoming you to Denton Reservoir.

7 Walk along the length of the stream towards the wooden fence panel at the end. Turn left on to the track and after 100m turn right into a field. It is not marked, but there is a broken stile and the path is used by walkers. Walk along the edge of the field with the hedge on your right. At the end, go into a second field and follow the well-trodden path diagonally across the field to the far end. Go through the gap in the hedge and follow the field edge to the stile.

8 Cross Denton Bridge and turn left, continuing to walk along the Grantham Canal for the next 2 miles until you reach the locks at Woolsthorpe. Turn left over the bridge and enjoy a rest at the canalside tables of the Dirty Duck.

PLACES OF INTEREST NEARBY

Grade I listed **Belvoir Castle** (pronounced 'Beaver') is home to the Duke and Duchess of Rutland and is open to visitors www.belvoircastle. com. Alternatively visit **Woolsthorpe Manor**, the birthplace of Sir Isaac Newton in 1642. The famous apple tree still stands in the manor orchard. www.nationaltrust.org.uk/woolsthorpe-manor.

Leaving Castle Bytham.

14 Castle Bytham to Clipsham

6.2 miles (10 km)

WALK HIGHLIGHTS

This walk stretches from Lincolnshire into Rutland, the smallest county in England. Castle Bytham is a beautiful stone village and the walk enters arable fields and meadows before reaching the striking stone village of Clipsham, explored before entering the woods. This walk is peaceful and charming, and best done in spring and summer when the fields are at their best.

THE PUB

The Olive Branch, Clipsham, **LE15 7SH**

This multi-award-winning eatery is set in a stunning village location and inside it reflects that character with an open fire and beams. In summer, the outside terrace in the beautiful garden makes a lovely alternative. Booking ahead is strongly recommended.

☎ 01780 410355 www.theolivebranchpub.com

THE WALK

1 From the High Street, turn into Church Lane which leads to a cemetery.

HOW TO GET THERE AND PARKING: There is off-road parking available in Castle Bytham and a parking bay on Station Road as you drive along the main road through the village. **Sat nav** NG33 4SQ.

MAP: OS Explorer 247 Grantham (GR SK 988184).

Follow the path around the cemetery before walking uphill past the old school. When you get to the cemetery gates, turn left, following the Danelaw Way sign past the cemetery, then through a wooden gate. Bear left, and continue to follow the trail through an enclosure of trees.

2 When you come to an opening which leads you into a field, bear left, walking diagonally across the field. At the end of this field, you reach an opening in the fence line. Cross the road and continue ahead through to the other side of the field towards a derelict building known as School Farm. Passing School Farm on your left, head across the field again, under the telegraph pole.

3 You reach a hedgerow with a waymarker on a post. Cross a small wooden bridge and enter the next field. Continue to walk directly across the field towards the telegraph poles. At the end of this field and to the left of the metal gate is a small wooden bridge with a Danelaw Way sign that leads through the hedge. The current footpath had been fenced off at this time, with access available to the right, following the hedge.

4 Continue ahead, with the fence on your right and when you reach the field, continue ahead. At the end of this field, cross the wooden bridge and continue ahead to a fence with a waymarker as you pass Holywell Quarry and walk through a wooded area.

5 At the end of this section, you pass a house and turn right onto the track. Continue ahead, passing through a gate and following the waymarker until you reach the gates at the end. Continue to follow this track as it bears left, uphill.

6 At the end of this track is a Rutland County Council waymarker. Follow this arrow directly across the field towards the house at the end. Cross

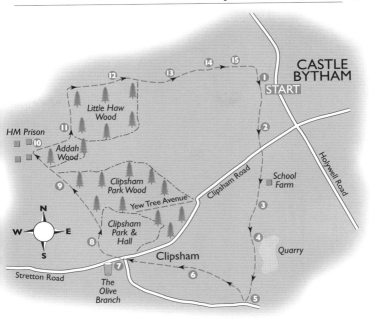

the field, and leave at the end through a gap in the fence and continue across a meadow towards a gate and onto the road in Clipsham.

7 At the signpost, head towards Stretton along the pavement. Bear left and head towards the Olive Branch.

8 From the Olive Branch, turn right out of the terrace and continue to follow the pavement. At the first junction, turn right and head along the road towards the church. As you continue past the village houses, the churchyard appears on your right and you pass a street sign to Bradley Lane. When you pass Clipsham Hall, bear left towards the farm building where there is a bridleway sign. Turn left.

9 Follow this tree-lined path which passes through a gate into a field. Bear left and follow the track round as it skirts into the next field. The hedge should be on your right. Walk ahead through the next field towards Addah Wood and again through the next field.

10 After this field and at the corner of the wood, turn left where there is a fallen post by a gap in the hedge for the public footpath. Then turn right, following the edge of Addah Wood. This path leads you into the woods at a waymarker.

11 The path through the woods passes HMP Stocken. Continue to follow the waymarkers along this winding trail. At the end of the woods is a metal gate into a field. Bear right and follow the edge of the wood.

12 Turn right at the end of the wood and walk downhill to the far right corner, by the waymarker on the hide. Here you go through a metal gate and cross a wooden bridge. Turn right at the footpath across the field.

13 Continue ahead, crossing fields for just over a mile, passing Little Haw Wood, where deer can often be seen. Waymarkers lead you as you follow the line of the ditch.

14 At the end of the ditch, continue ahead through a field towards a copse. At the end of this field, cross the fence at the waymarker and follow the track towards the dismantled railway which takes you through a disused tunnel and out towards a fence. Cross the stile by the waymarker and turn right. The fence line should be on your right.

15 From the edge of this field, continue ahead into a meadow along the trodden path. When you reach a stile at a road, turn right and walk towards Castle Bytham, following the road as it bears left at the top. You finish your walk through the village.

PLACES OF INTEREST NEARBY

Burghley House is a stunning, privately owned, Elizabethan mansion which sits in vast grounds and parkland. House tours are available, as well as tearooms. www.burghley.co.uk.

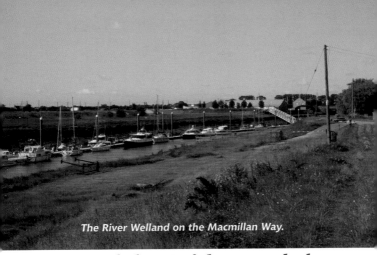
The River Welland on the Macmillan Way.

15 Fosdyke Bridge and the River Welland

5.5 miles (8.8 km)

WALK HIGHLIGHTS

The Fens is a traditionally flat and marshy region in Lincolnshire. Most of the fens were drained centuries ago, resulting in a series of drainage channels and man-made rivers and dykes. This walk shows a prettier side to what one may expect, and it is a great introduction to the fens. The riverside walk along the Macmillan Way takes you to quiet country lanes and crosses arable fields before following the leafy footpath back.

THE PUB

The Ship Inn, Fosdyke Bridge **PE12 6LH**
This dog-friendly pub has a cosy atmosphere inside and serves good food in a friendly environment.
☎ 01205 260764 www.shipinnfosdyke.com

HOW TO GET THERE AND PARKING: From Holbeach take the A17 north to Fosdyke Bridge. Parking is available for patrons at the Ship Inn on the southern bank of the river. There is roadside parking available north of the river beyond the Fosdyke Yacht Haven. **Sat nav** PE20 2DD.

MAP: OS Explorer 249 Spalding & Holbeach (GR TF 319322).

THE WALK

1 From the Ship Inn, turn right and cross the bridge. Pass Fosdyke Yacht Haven and turn right by the bridleway sign following the grassy bank which runs alongside the yacht harbour. At the end of this track you reach a hamlet of houses. Turn right, through the gate with the waymarkers and begin to walk alongside the River Welland on the Macmillan Way.

2 This section of the Macmillan Way is 2¾ miles long and passes typical Fen landscapes. This raised path has views of arable fields on your left and the river gradually bears away towards the Fosdyke Wash. It is a good area to watch birds and wildlife.

3 The path reaches the end by Kirton Marsh pumping station, where there is a public footpath sign. Continue ahead, over the stile and leave the Macmillan Way. Follow the flat path towards a fence at the end. Climb the stile and turn left at the footpath.

4 Pass a white farmhouse and follow the track as it curves round, passing a large barn where you bear right onto a farm track. Continue to follow this track until you reach a T-junction and bear right.

5 At the end of this track, walk past the farmhouse, leaving by the white barrier. Turn left onto Low Mill Lane, following the signpost for Fosdyke.

6 After ½ mile, leave the lane on the bend and turn left, where there is a footpath sign. Walk between two hedgerows until you reach an opening into an arable field. Turn right, keeping the hedge line on your right.

7 At the end of this field, you reach a track on a bend. Cross it and continue

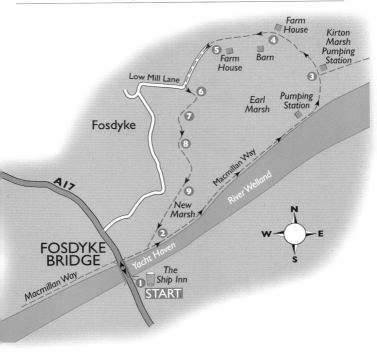

ahead where the path gradually begins to bear left. Continue until you reach a white metal gate on your left by a footpath sign. Climb the raised bank here to follow it. This first section of footpath may seem overgrown in places. If so, you can walk along the track for a few metres where there is a secondary path trodden down by walkers.

8 Continue to follow this marked footpath back towards Fosdyke Bridge. At the end of this first footpath, you reach a track. Bear right, cross the track, and after 10m go straight back onto the footpath on your left.

Varying fen landscapes at point 8.

9 Continue to follow this footpath which eventually comes out at an opening beside the River Welland where you started. Follow the path back to the gate and turn left, following the track that runs behind a series of houses. At the end is the busy A17, turn left and walk towards the Ship Inn.

PLACES OF INTEREST NEARBY

The **RSPB Frampton Marsh Nature Reserve**, with plenty of nature walks, wildlife to observe and a pleasant picnic area, will appeal to adults and children alike. Alternatively visit **The Bubble Car Museum** at Langrick, perfect for car or retro enthusiasts. The museum houses a large display of bubble cars, offers rides and also has a café. www.bubblecarmuseum.co.uk.